I0141705

Una Woods was born and raised in Belfast, Ireland, where she now lives. A seminal influence on her writing was the atmosphere of the city road where she spent her early years, with its imposing three-storey terraced houses and black factory smoke and the streets around where children gathered to play their seasonal games. In stark contrast to this, the other key source of early awakenings was the rich green countryside around her Grandmother's house in Co Down where she and her family spent all of the school holidays.

In terms of her writing, at a certain point it became clear to her that in early consciousness lay the essence of what she had to say: 'The early years are a faith of impressions; memory in its pure form; the future all-sensed, the vital source of the present. Everything we see was first seen there, the signs are a landscape that reappears. It's sudden'.

First published poems and short stories appeared
in the 1980's in the New Writing Page of The
Irish Press, edited by David Marcus.
The Dark Hole Days, a novella and short stories
was published by Blackstaff Press in 1984.
Over the years stories and poems have appeared in
anthologies in Ireland, The UK and USA.

Other Una Woods books published by Ashtrees are:
Afternoons, selected poems, 2006.
Mr and Mrs McKeown- the accidental maze, a novella,
2010.
An icicle for an eye, notepoems, 2011.
2 Plays, Grace before meals; For want of the call, 2013.
Splintered vision, selected poems, 2016

The ordinary of the disquiet

Published by Ashtrees

2021

ashtreespress@gmail.com

ISBN: 978-1-8384318-0-8
All rights reserved

To Tony

what shimmers
is the ordinary of
the disquiet
March moves
to faint fragments
no-man's paradise
about to spring

rose-tinted rose
scent of all scents
proof that promise
is pure promise
and memory doesn't
ask for proof

illegible January
slowing dusk
through branches separated
amongst themselves
intermittent rustle of
red-eyed traffic
past the railinged gate
closed to all
but who live there or
know the code

hill upon hill
the distance
pressed up against
time after time
not able to reach
what is already reached

the low cottages
suntrap of the crossroads
whichever way you go
you'll be burned
by whitewashed walls

not the lough
the sun's icy glitter
for summer play
the stones were too hard
to walk on anyway
now there's a reflection
on the slapping water
there's today
time paddles in it
it splashes on the overlapping
waves
you could walk on stones
and feel only
their roots

when a voice
called out
in the evening street
the name it called
was absence
(it sounded like Kathleen}

and the message
from the night clouds
closing over the navy city sky –
nobody has a god-given right
to the apparition

dusk chirrs in

across rooftops

a slow swoop

on houses

nightjar of the city

it is rare to see

the moment it

appears out of the

failing light

it is a slice of

flight

cut from the

atmosphere

there is the odd trill

of thinning traffic

silhouettes on the road

look startled by

streetlight

a girls' choir
round mouthed
like an orchard
of cherry apples
chosen by bees
the whimsy of the Assumption
in the swirl of a city cloudbreak
a flight of pigeons
you defined by the
closeness of their wings
to the sun
then everything burned
in the flames of a feeling
for seasons or
a ball thrown high into
the long-eveninged street

jewel of isolation afar glistens

a field snow packed with a late

sun-thistle

the day's quiet manoeuvre

creeps across the countryside

the white cottages settle in

to their religious differences

the twilight lowing of a cow comes

from an extreme need

consciousness has

through the hall window

the day brightened

as if the beginning

was just beginning

and all future direction

was the road to the river

reeds risk
the bend of
the river
there is depth
down there
you climb out
of it
but too late
it has seen you

voices
oiled the darkness
in the big yard
in aloof blue
the moonfields
rose beyond the
empty road
that twisted and fell to
 the invisible town
if that was the future
it was good enough

white clouds whisper
across this silent blue sky
the tip of the telephone mast
was made for days
like this

November light
the dying light the light
dying to light the last ray
stranded on tudor eaves the gate
a-clink the rusting leaves, the maple leaves
a magpie picks among
flies away with a piece of gold
to where-
the shadows drop lamplight grows
the hiddenness of all the old
years

the fanlight
fetched home
from the hopeless
and pasted it
above the door

the early effort
to inhabit intermittence, discovering
there was no continuity
to alive

the night shop
grit in the desert
a few lost steps
out of nowhere
a silhouette afar
is sorting potatoes
in a dusty sack

in the world of

worlds a pink ice-cream

sun stone-lifts a wall

just opposite the

pier road

boulders are loosened to

multiply along the

wet shore

seagulls scream in wild

scraps of flight

seaweed is the smell

of out of all doors

and still definitions recede

into the vast

of a pony's trot

on the high road

what do you think

you are doing? someone asked

the child, not knowing

the question (if ever valid)

was at least years away

nothing, the child answered,

hiding the thing she didn't think

she was doing, then added,

and now I think I'm going out to play

a tinge of streetlight

on a parlour

no effort to stop

the day from failing

a piano note

plays alone

there is something far

from over

from the road
the slant
of a hall door
inner light
is an angle
on the illusion
of being at home

the bang of a door
in a row of houses
a figure steps out
onto a path
pauses
in that pause after the bang
all night roads
are walked

the troubled sound of
the helicopter circling
above houses changed the
air of the suburban street
but no more than the
single thrush calling from
the evening garden tree

when you raced to
the entry mouth and
looked down the street
you were looking for
no less than the
answer to everything
but the girl with her
own rope tied tightly
around the top of the lamppost
had already found and
taken possession of it

the shop door
tinkled deep
within someone hoked
among treasure
on the threshold
winter sharpened its
gleam an instant before
the tinkle blurred the
measure of all outside
and in

    lamplight
    halfway
    down the street
    standing at the top
    you hesitated
    to make up your mind or
    so you thought

faith
the church bell
founded its own

the passerby
in the failing light
was a guess
that got it right
outside
the net-curtained
bay window

a fanlight's half-hidden
glimmer
as if someone left a note
folded on the step
saying
wait here forever

Kenmare thrush

The fragile thrush
prickling with existence
dusk's camouflage, a silent glow-
worm spreads on the damp grass
from unearthly still to little startled
hops then as if by a trick of the third eye
the thrush has flown and imperceptibly
darkness is there
for a moment the immensity of things
sits frozen
then observation, the resort of human
dwelling, moves away
from the window

pale pink roses
buttoned on the scent
of arrival
the archway is pure
suggestion
the path a lapel
to pin it on
in a cobweb of
pebble-dash ivy climbs
to reach its evergreen
is tangled in coats that hang
just inside the open door
hall shadows deep in the chime
of the Grandfather clock

who knew the ants were
single minded scurrying in
and out of garden stones
voices said this and that
the path wound to a purpose
footsteps would forget under
the stones the ants carried
on building the pyramids

fail
is a word
that glistens
with possibility
lamplight failed
to light the street

up the road
on the Sunday walk
past the giant's foot
where clay grew pale
wildflowers and
grass was the broken heart
of stones, then as if the city
had no mercy at all
two graveyards astride
a Sunday park

  the time it took
  for the black clock
  on the black mantelpiece
  to come back from afar
  and find the same afternoon
  ticking away

the town clock
announced the world
hour
over the soul of
the cathedral bell
the age of reason
was a surprise of clover
at the top of the field

the river
never runs
its course
it runs and runs
at its shallow part
children play there
knowing the world
is transparent

Autumn leaves
fluttered from the notes
of the black piano
then the long winter
of parlour and other
extremes

the whinny of corn
in the river field
the bridge is stopped
at stone grey
what's glimpsed up the hill
of the road opposite
a figure fetched by sunlight
to the door of a low cottage
the feeling of leaving
closer and closer

the figure
at the night corner
with its tiny sucked-in
ashglow
knew what planet
it was living on

in winter's whacked cold
on the convent playing
field
shouts seemed a victory
for life long after
school

stand out
on the winter road
it's the ideal place
if freezing is
the future dream

on the frailgrey
road
a revelation
vanishment
is dust one
minute

the ladybird
an ecstasy of
global dots
you could look at
the earth
from outer space
and still stand on
the garden path

footsteps, crinkled
branches, hand-twined
in a terrace of trees
rushes of air, copperfastened
voices, leaf-peppered
repeat
the future has no flesh
but the fall of these
passing footsteps

just before dusk
the light
luminous
as if the word fail
is far
fetched

now as you turned
left onto the road
to the river
the road ahead (the one you
didn't take) stretched further
into another day, sunlight
streaking the far horizon,
where you would turn left
and take the road to the river

deep in the fir tree

the coo-coo of the woodpigeon

a dark place to go

sunlight flickers on

needles it sharpens

its edge on the suspense of

the woodpigeon's call

there is a standoff

for a moment the sun

will not go in

nor the woodpigeon

come out

just as the light starts to fail

there is a loud flapping

the back door opens

into the kitchen

in the half light
bagpipes play
long notes
squeezed out through
the walls of the white cottage
to become stars
not yet discovered
by the sky
silence spreads across
the darkening fields
one person's private air
is another's stargazing

sitting at the top
of the high field
a lull in play
summer stared at you
as if to say
you can't keep up
with a lovely day

the blue sky
above the rocks
a flag
that flew the possibility
life could be celebrated
as one fine day
and the future
would wave it

the robin
pecked at crumbs
on the snowy windowsill
up behind
the orchard trees were
tufted with white
all the air
was a glassy blue
it froze   you froze
something you knew completely
you didn't know

and through the window
through the still-leafed
tree the lighter light
of distance
a white building, just in view
seaside white in seaside light
if light alone
is the measure of possibility

winter road again
white fields
start of red sunset on
low horizon
white-topped headstones
glow in the small churchyard
ahead
footsteps quicken
up the icy hill
cheeks aglow
to reach the fading
words in stone

leaf-jewels
sparkled in march
sunlight
blue diamonded sky
shines between branches
ice-summered high
you see
but today what is not seen
is nowhere to be said

from the fernfield
farther fields misted
into distant hills
one long summer's day
some unknown expanse
seemed on display
all the day's play
was at a standstill
and faith for its unknown sake
was asked of you
to keep on the road home
the light already fading

the green breath
of deep grass
there grasshoppers live
in flicky harmony
the long hill
down to the gate its
dreamy iron shiver every
now and then
who is coming up the hill
the future a slow earthy
quake behind them

the scene is
a deep gleam
on the edge of a
gorge
there are flowers
wild and flimsy
down the side
smoke from a
chimney someone has
built a house down there
how did they get to
believe they could
climb out of
somebody else's view

an old car receded slowly
down the long country road
suddenly
a warm wide day
didn't know its own
limits but
the silence after
was everywhere
you turned

the sun's blank stare
in a back yard
a cobweb shimmered
on rough brick
someone dropped a metal
bin-lid in another yard
you were closer
than you thought

the bounce of a ball
off the gable wall
life was one
repetitive evening
but if you caught it
you were in

the sun-yellow dare
of ragweeds in the field
across the road
a step there and you'll be
too close to the sickle's
silver ray

this patchy cream-memoried
sky
spiked with dark-blown
leaves
an idea the country lane had
once (through a straggly hedge
the far gleam of blue-guessed
mountains)
this scrappy high-lit city
sky
shredded by tall branches
stole the idea out of pure
need to remember its place

the sound of a door
closing down the evening
street
you weren't ready
for that

a small town station
just as the train pulled away
on the outward journey
charging into the distance
how much were you in charge
then fell into the rhythm of
the moving train
the chug, chug of destination
mixed up with a dream

       reality
       the word
       a hard sparkle
       on things
       lived parallel
       to the ground

it was only
a minute ago
the roses gathered
around the gate
and you swung it
behind you

heat waved
on the rising field
and light squinted
at a green glaze
there were butterflies
barely bothered on flowers
and women's talk desultory
on the loose-stoned path
every now and then a noise
echoed from inside the house
like a clock ticking
on a summer trance

this weak-willed
early April afternoon
    the sky
    has no idea
the wind can barely
bring itself to rouse
the lazy-leafed trees
season is a pale shade
of its winter self
imagination is a figment
of the imagination

the sound of the
city door
closed a way of
life a minute ago
had seemed the
possibility of a stop and
start of noise
the road outside had
yet to decide

sweet pea
the bashful side
of the wall
snapdragons
nettles bold
a garden gap
run wild
with one after the other
through

details fell
into disrepair
on the dusk road
nothing
could be fixed
but the stars
were tools that took
their time
to come out
of the chimney smoke

telephone wings
swallows' wires
traffic driven by
a rush of air
houses swum in a shallow
pink pond
you were out of school
but little did you know
that day's lesson

look at the eyes
of the blackbird
be blinded
by clarity
crumbs can't come
to your defence

haystacks
hills
the slow half-light
barns that settle
in a big yard
sawdust shreds a
glimmer of light
voices gradually let
go of their said
where cows munch slowly
the silver-bladed quiet

        unison of psalms
        from the nuns' private
        chapel
        pure acoustics
        voice isolated
        silence personified
        then out to the road
        where it was all
        of a muchness
        beyond you

a pearl of
private evening
on the light-peeped
road
gleams on a corner
a figure uncrowded
by the day
tucked away down
the adjoining street
a wild patch
hides its daisies and
buttercups
among bits of last night's
coloured bottles

isolation's heels
down the pale-eveninged
street
click into ahead
where an appointment
fills the air and
anticipation isolated
is a meeting

a shout from
nowhere on the
midnight road
called you out
but it was dark and
you were willing yourself
 into a dream
which way would you go

dew-frost
the rooster's cold call
the world is
morning's fault
across the fields, get up
the mad cows
have broken down the ditch
and wandered off

the farmer pitched hay
in the late summer field
prickled with sun it fell
loosely into a haystack
a needle caught firelight
in an autumn city parlour
before sewing a button
on a heavy winter coat

Easter 2020

the day is becoming
undone
something outside of
its control
Easter rises alone
on the fire-blackened mountain
nobody is allowed
to go there
there is a leafy smouldering
in the empty suburbs
all outside is a decree of
the ominous
in the room a single
tiny fly is circling the books
you could easily miss it

on the front of

the road

the strange light

foretold strange times

the man at his gate stared

it in the face

the factory women in

bright scarves opposite

the sepia light

in his eyes

their laughs he took

to heart

later by the fireside

he wondered to himself

about life

the primrose grew

partly responsible for

the solitary road

moon
monstrance of the night

rises in full bright
isolation

disperses differences
below

the black sky a
chapel of illusion
carved out of old
devotions

light slithers
down on houses

roofs glisten
with dusk-trail

figures fetched
into their elsewhere

eke out the road
in another life's day

as you were carrying
your cross
up the agony of the
side aisle
the cleaning woman
raised her mop and
yelled at you to get
out
she'd just washed it

A walk in the woods

there's a crackling
in the woods
a twilight sound
a twig makes
when light streaks down
through the trees
birdsong is a high breaking
of the heart of silence
people whisper
in the woods   trees are
unwritten books in an illegible
library
suddenly
a rustling in the undergrowth
not for borrowing

light
the closed eye

no
a little more

else why
all those fields

roads
the passerby

all that future
still

tree
through the window

please tell
what day it is

leaves, reveal
your trembling season

gleam, paint mottled light's
inscrutable hour

collared dove, just please
don't fly away

a tin can
kicked down
the night entry
rolled emptily a bit
then stopped, glinted
on the cold ground
under the sky's spread-out
glitter
steel heel-tips diminished
down the long entry
a yard door shook a bit
then abruptly closed

commandments
garden stones
don't stray from the
path that leads all
round the house and
back to the garden
stones- now mind not to
fall over into the
flowers

as if there was
no sound before
the piper played
silver notes stretched
across the fields
as if there was no
light before twilight
only the long rays
struck the grass
and the piper played
away as if there was nowhere
before somewhere else

yes
you walked
the open country roads
the hilly backroads
the tangled laneways
but did you prove it?

piano notes
in an evening parlour
some heavenly body
of music above
a front door opens to
a road that runs round
to the sound of a street
ahead
a line of girls skipping
a flat chant
calls you in

the sun disappeared
behind a cloud
proving the high field
had no will of its own
and playing there
was pointless

faint is far
the better word
for here
away over the fields
the townlands
sprinkle

and still the word

evades sight

a glimmer of faith

is not even close

and still the spire

rises

just out of sight

into the

clear blue sky

the will

of a bee's buzz

to lead summer

up the garden path

where the monkey puzzle

waits in the corner shade

a street lamp
an empty bus-stop
if you can survive that
you can survive
 a street lamp
 an empty bus-stop

how to live
the flutter of a butterfly
on a garden path
one minute you thought
you could
the next you were running
for the rocky height
of the field across the road

there is no proof
of alive
but the effort to follow
  the memory
   in front of you

late afternoon
city road
white squares
drawn on pavement
hop, jump, beyond
the powdery periphery
into the chalked world
a careful game
is going on

the first faith
you followed
was the atmosphere
of the city road
as if a fickle air
could be an eternal truth

the scrape of a tyreless
wheelbarrow
on the hard pavement
in the deep of a night
was a future ripped
from a stranger's dream

the street's chest sank
when the sun dipped
behind a cloud
suddenly a ball
had a flat bounce
and for a pavement to
lift it was twice the effort

    the pink pebble-
    dash
    of a seaside house
    is pure guess
    at an ideal life

a stony beach

a cold blast of

grey air

the sea chops at

the shore's hard edge

children run wild

over the top of

dead-grass dunes

all in good time

it will be

a victorious holiday

The day's end

When the pink sky
mixed the fine rise of
smoke with the smell of
a log fire and fields
folded away their dandelions
for the day and the nearby town
fell further back
from the hilly road
the children came home
from the river in single
file scuffing their loose-tied shoes
along the low ditch by the
roadside

        someone shouted
        in the night street
        and suddenly
        there was more
        to it

the hen-run clucked
in the mid-afternoon sun
the brown earth scratched
idly at the edges of grass
from inside the nearby house
delft hit the frailty
of delft
something stirred
at the centre of
how long was there to go

     out of the shadows
     light flickered
     across the night yard
     as if an oil lamp carried
     was the next best thing
     to no-one

it was such a small thing
the light through a crack
in the chapel door
it escaped in
you escaped out
but it was the crack
that kept faith
with itself

between day
and night
a quiet word is
unheard
on the hall-lit threshold
it is not repeated

fireworks
crack of mist
on the city road
a sparkler in the
hand of a child
who believes the
dancing fizzle is a fact
and a way to look at
drab entry walls
eyes fixed on the
sputtering blaze
even as sparks jump
on bare skin

who thinks
they know
doesn't know
what to think

Glass flowers

the flowers
might break free
from the glass vase
their thin stems
might shatter the
garden illusion
city traffic shudders
the glass window
you didn't know
back in the country
fragile stems tweaked in
the breeze
butterflies fell on expelled
petals the tractor was fitful
in the high field
voices on paths were splinters
of what was said in summer

plumes of city
rising to fall
on everyday words
there was no reason
why there was every
reason
the city settled back
to an unearthly siren
then walked through
the debris one side to
the other

he stood in the
night shop
the dark street could
not touch him
he was deep within his
own corner light
a few words with
a customer
the soft bell of the till
down the street
young people were
careless around a
street lamp

the gospel
a word that
was bright with
city truths
the feel of a new
missal
pages like flimsy
prayers to every good Friday
Latin a shiny code
a weightless wonder to be
carried up the road

Painting

the brush strokes
stopped into sudden depth
thick blurbs pushed into
impressions of places
oily blues, greens
 a rough road winding
to where you couldn't see
the artist's
complete absence

Judgement

go to the edge
of the peninsula
watch from a height
the gannets in a busy sun
diving
there is a boat
far out
moving so slow
on the wide sea
you have to stand
at speed
to stay on dry land

the north sun
westering the low
sky a chit of a
ray on a cold land
it's sudden
a breath you could
see a seagull of a
swoop
a white flap on a rocky
height
the north is
a quick-felt thing

in long strides
he bit the dusk
with each step
the day was swallowed
into his strangeness
he saw no one
left or right
in his far fixed
eyes somewhere
only he could go
muttering into his
world if he looked
back the day he hadn't
known would disappear

a woman stood
on her front step
long into evening
her eyes restless moved
up and down the fading street
then settled on the house opposite
its door closed on a fanlit hall
children played in the
middle of the road, back and
forth till lamps came on
they laughed when the
woman said
have yous no homes
to go to?

the factory horn foretold

long silence

the sound a deafening eternity

it wasn't timeless

though for a moment after it stopped

it was

that was a relief

in this place jewelled

with expanse

void is the heart

 of all that beats

 ahead is a path

 that leads to suspense

 if you stand on the

  midnight country

  road and no-one speaks

the steeple stands
high on its own
it is a rock built for
seagulls to circle
faith is a wild height
looked at from the ground
a blustery sunlit cloud
passes by
down in the chapel
the consecration bell
rings in captivity
outside the seagull's cry
circles the steeple

The west

landscape of the west
wide, rough
few-peopled
an eye cast over
a remote longing
an ancient kind
of belonging
the west is a wilderness
in the veins
an exile etched
on a left behind air
there is a blood sun
that seeps down
the heights of the west
are its home
there is no undercity
of lost light there

the prayers of the
faithful a low drone
on a long aisle
something had to
give
the light on the
altar was deep within
but then there was another
light imperceptible
a golden stream
it ran free
over the thick pews
over the murmuring
sound, private it was
a running commentary
over a view

light gleamed out

from a late yard

where someone

worked on unsayable

things

old broken things

you couldn't say

what they once were

except that they were

whole

could they be restored?

a rhetorical hammering

breaks the night silence

the crows' ragged calls

down at the bend of

the country road

a high blue sky

a chaos of black

wings

in and out of tall

incurious trees

you couldn't hear

the crows without

seeing the road

turn sharply

beyond the bend

from concealed to loudly

concealed

National Concert Hall

there is a strangeness
on things
it won't be beaten
a dazzle on the concert
hall a car sits
outside a hotel
lobby through the glass
door life swings into
evening they should have
left for the journey home
who knows when the queue
of people will get in to hear
the music
is a celestial symphony
of rubber tyres
on the road

on the other side
of the entry wall
where cement grows
pigeons
there is no
need to think they
have nowhere to fly
even if the brick light
raises a wall that gives
nothing back but
bread becoming crumbs

the cow's low
from the evening
field
like an unsettlement
over
your own decision

in the dusty room
for want of brushing
(so the dust might settle
somewhere else) the sun
was an exposure
of the middle of things
afternoon
a floor
a motionless summer
a sudden shout
might confirm only
the distance of a street
still running feet
sent dust flying

Garden of Eden

everything was lovely
in the summer garden
but you weren't allowed
to touch the flowers
or the apples in the orchard
trees
still the time before you knew
is yours

the definite light
in the barn doorway
it had a future
business a
thriving optimism
the big yard concentrated
all its activities there
it was quick
but if you joined it
you were a life member

act out
the twilight
it doesn't commit
to light to dark
its glimmer is smart
luring rooftops
to a silvery in between
playing with the idea
of a permanent way out of
the darkening road

if you put all
your effort into
a shop light
what did you expect
when it was turned
off the day being
over for good

city wasteland
it tried hard
even growing
shiny green blades
of glass
that reflected
last nights songs
of freedom

they gathered at the
corner they were
company for each
other
smoke reached up
from a terrace of houses
it had the same uncanny
idea
voices animated around
a blazing fire you'd never
know by morning ashes

voices in the street
far off tongues
tied to what could not
be heard
the club door had no way
through
it was an ajar dark
you never knew
what was inside
you didn't know
you didn't need to know
except what was a glimpse
of being in

what effort
the faint rumble
of traffic
from another road

on the solemn terraced
road grey after the
war they never spoke
a gramophone turned, tightened
then burst into a small far voice
squeezed into an old
song that travelled to a
future guessed by children
the past scraped round on a
pinhead in a parlour that had
quiet in its crackles

the dash of whin
among the rocks
as if a sun could
rise on any earth there
was shouting that someone
was found or had simply
stopped running in the
middle of a breath there
were sounds over the field
they could end in the city
where the streets had hard
winters and fanlights and whin-
yellow street lamps and running
over kerbs that could be rocks
in the newly exiled mind

Road trip

a middle place where
you have left what is behind
and not arrived at what
is ahead
you're simply on it
on your way
there is the wheel sound
on tarmac like some permanent
spinning round
eyes fixed on the road ahead
is part of the trip
at times a daze
the quick thrill of passing
landscapes
yet there is an easy feeling of
just driving midway
you can't do anything about
behind or ahead it's a sort
of meditation a freedom from
ends
you have no sense of getting into
or out of the car

the fire roared in
the grate it was the
fire of winter
you could go anywhere with
that fire in your head
all you needed was the
cold in your soul

the traffic hummed
on the roundabout
a chorus of brown autumn
it affirmed the life the
swallows knew gathered
on the high September wire
the readiness to flutter then
lift off because the air was
right they didn't think
about departure

down the dank dim
street a mist only a
city could make houses
stuck to old times
lamplight
the nothing you knew
had a yellow tinge it
stopped with itself
going beyond itself
to a glow

on the corner of
the pier road the
shop was crammed
with trinkets they were
the life you would
choose being every
colour and having a
lightness a sparkle
you had the will to
be a trinket in the winter
city then steam grew heavy
as the train squeezed into
the night station

someone called
your name in the
street and
you had one chance
to prove it was
you

stars
   hailstones that
   hit the sky
   what doesn't melt
   void is decorated
   with the word
   winter is written in
   icicles hanging from
   low roofs the country
   yard is an ice-brimmed
   barrel   voices freeze
   where light huddles
   round a small window

in the scrapyard
a remnant sun
picked out old
things there was
a sound of hammering
you could hear it
across the city streets
not everything can be
fixed even in the country
yard an axe is heard falling
 in the afternoon sun and
there is something that's
not the stretching fields
that has no completion

a thin layer of snow
on a city pavement
dark figures are carried
along by numb
there is no sound on
the road but the silence
is a removed one, a strange one
it is not the loss of a day's
noise it is its own thing
an icing skimmed off vast
standing out on the cold
white road the only feeling is
not dwelling on things

looking across the side
field from the shadow of
the big fir tree just
inside the gate and where
the henrun above had gone
quiet the hens being settled
on their night perches the
light from the new garage
forecourt was an activity
you were ready for the
boy working there appearing
out of it

atmosphere can't be
said you can take its
word for it
roads fall for it they
rise the air is a sudden
rush after a bus stops
a fidgety dust is afternoon's
business the world is a
rumour people spread
outside the shops deep in
who did what
look at the sun peeking from
brick on the far side of the road

there's just that feeling
of participation
it's almost overwhelming
an enthrallment started
by opening a door to the
front of a road
transient it's a certain
time of the day everything
seems at its height
possibility needs no
development it is deep
within itself and lightly
fulfills its future the passing
world is suffused with a hum
that is its own intention of
making a noise

Donegal

the road wound down
to the village it was the
winding down houses
dotted on slopes of green
hills all around patches of
fields bordered by low
stone walls, turf the new
scent of amazement caught
the breath of clear air
rising
looking across at the
open land it was in
expectation of days like
this the winding down to
the widening out
again and again

the distracted stars

they mix up distance

with the city road they

are careless with a sky that

has black lament in its

night there is smoke from the

chimneys on the upward terrace

figures walk in the middle of the

footpath, they don't look

up they are distracted by

what is behind and what

is ahead

the country women
on the garden path
leant over the stones
to examine the flowers
calling them by their
names
details the bee ignored
its buzz honoured
approaching, retreating
and the children played
they were fully within
the buzz
 not feeling the sting of a past
 or future on their skin

October 2020

a single autumn tree outside
the window it doesn't know
all past autumns come to life in its
leaves a large golden tabernacle it
houses the still blue
grey of this lonely Sunday
suddenly sunlight brings it
to itself on the surface it is a
dazzle of gold on gold display
it doesn't know
beyond the autumn birth of a
tree
the invisible city
is dying

a little light is still left in the
day the low hills dip in
pale sunlight smoke points
out cottages across the
townlands a mirage of grass
glistens the odd car putters
along the winding road the
human race ekes out another day
gates are opened for beasts to
tramp to night fields there is
such a thing as frozen time there
is the way frost turns dew into
fixed eyes there is who is
seeing and who is seen

Dreams

they came to the stones from the village
hard as stones the sea glistened over
wind-cold summer skin-blue wildness
in their legs they bounded over rocks
exposed in their bones, city children
streets cemented with hearts that had
winter in their bones followed the village
children, followed the wind, freedom yelled
it yelled as if it could be caught like
gasps of seasurf whins like displaced
buttercups on a desert mountain
the path leading up to the white cottage,
city children, holiday children
rambled, a midnight terraced road
back in their winter dreams ahead
they would dream free to walk on
the cold wet stones over the wild
seaweed to the salt-cry of the sea
village children with the village children
but what did the village children dream?

things will seem as they
are there was a first
time it was before the
chapel chimed in with its
voice of sin seeming had more
reason being simply what
was when you looked up the
road and saw the sun baptise
a cusp of pavement   it seemed infinite
and belief in some pure form it had no
commandment and no confession
it seemed incense sprinkled on a transient
world only dusk could question it and
dusk was sprinkled with street lights

coming down the mountainside

the airport road

a winding shelf above the

precarious city

arrival falls off, scatters below

a shining sprawl of lights

a home-packed

Christmas view

being away grew

out of the troubles-ragged landscape

beyond the scrappy barbed

wire the Kings Hall clock stood

down among the lit houses from

the height of the night mountain road a

new-tucked notion of home

Time

it seems from the outset
you chose mid-time or it
chose you so the past is in
the middle of now, now is in
the middle of the future which is
in the middle of the past no matter
what you know
of years that flew you must stick
with this mid-point view if you
go to either side of it you will lose
your balance and fall off now and time
will have dominion

girls are waiting for country
boys to come home from
the town they're sitting on
the high stone garden wall
as if being seen is the be all
of everything these are new
times they have done their
running through fields, no more
climbing trees or jumping from
grassy heights everything attunes
to dignity they will sit and smile
and when the time is right there
will be meetings at the crossroads
and another day they will walk
away as if it's nothing

hares on the hill
endued onto the cold
mist they are there
sudden their ears blades
of alert they dart down
out of sight in the morning
field dew-eyes multiply
on cold grass
there are children in the
lower swamp they had come
looking for cows they forgot
when the mist-sudden hares
appeared on the morning
hill

the hour goes back today
it goes back to the hour that called
the city road to light its halls
when dusk was still day only
the light lower while children
still played in the smoky streets like
magic deserts lantern-lit you could
make anything up around five o'clock
the mystery of the clock that chimed
in the country hall at last becoming
Christmas

the pantomime lights
dimmed then out to
the dark winter streets
there were two choices-
make up life, light it up
or aim to be in the pantomime

voices in the white field
stopped in a daze silence
packs the air it is thick with
everywhere at once what
sinks in, the surface freezes
there are words like glitter,
gleam, life words
a bursting of breath into the
white atmosphere
say what you like
it too will be frozen

tall stark-sticked winter
tree   through it
the sky wisp-blue
grey
late January
4 pm
it's not a description

moon-break

on the crossroads

the whole earth is shoved

into forked space

vast is a clock on the

dot of elsewhere

silence, wide awake

rises to an abyss of fields

there is an ordered blue

over the large untidy

shadows of the corner trees

the fanlight is lit above ´

the country door

and still –

www.ingramcontent.com/pod-product-compliance
Lightning Source LLC
Chambersburg PA
CBHW071006040426
42443CB00007B/686